Pebble™ Plus

A Visit to

The Library

by B. A. Hoena

Consulting Editor: Gail Saunders-Smith, Ph.D.
Reading Consultant: Jennifer Norford, Senior Consultant
Mid-continent Research for Education and Learning
Aurora, Colorado

Capstone press

Mankato, Minnesota

Pebble Plus is published by Capstone Press
151 Good Counsel Drive, P.O. Box 669, Mankato, Minnesota 56002
http://www.capstonepress.com

1 2 3 4 5 6 09 08 07 06 05 04

Library of Congress Cataloging-in-Publication Data
Hoena, B. A.
    The library/by B. A. Hoena.
    p. cm.—(Pebble Plus, A visit to)
    Includes bibliographical references and index.
    Contents: The library—Using the library—Librarians—Checking out—Learning at the library.
    ISBN 0-7368-2394-8 (hardcover)
    1. Public libraries—Juvenile literature. [1. Public libraries. 2. Libraries.] I. Title. II. Series.
Z665.5.H64 2004
027.4—dc22   2003011993

Editorial Credits

Sarah L. Schuette, editor; Jennifer Bergstrom, series designer; Karen Risch, product planning editor

Photo Credits

Capstone Press/Gary Sundermeyer, cover (girl, shelf), all interior photos
PhotoDisc Inc., cover (computer)

Pebble Plus thanks the St. Peter Public Library, St. Peter, Minnesota, for the use of its library for photo shoots.

Note to Parents and Teachers

The series A Visit to supports national social studies standards related to the production, distribution, and consumption of goods and services. This book describes and illustrates a visit to a public library. The images support early readers in understanding the text. The repetition of words and phrases helps early readers learn new words. This book also introduces early readers to subject-specific vocabulary words, which are defined in the Glossary. Early readers may need assistance to read some words and to use the Table of Contents, Glossary, Read More, Internet Sites, and Index/Word List sections of the book.

Word Count: 121
Early-Intervention Level: 13

Table of Contents

The Library

The library is a busy place to visit. Many people use the library every day.

The library is filled with shelves. Each shelf holds many books.

Juvenile
Non-Fiction

001 - 394.268 ➡

⬅ 394.269 - 551.499

Using the Library

Library visitors do research.
They use computers and
books to look for information.

To use this
computer, take
your library card
to the check out
desk to sign up

Visitors sit quietly.

Some read books for fun.

Other visitors study.

Librarians

The library has many books to read. Librarians help visitors find the right book.

CHECK OUT

Librarians read picture
books during storytime.
Children and adults listen
to the story.

Checking Out

Visitors can check out, or borrow, books for a few weeks. A library clerk scans the visitor's library card.

Children's Area

The library has many
other materials to check out.
Visitors borrow movies,
magazines, and CDs.

Learning

A library is a good place
to read and learn.

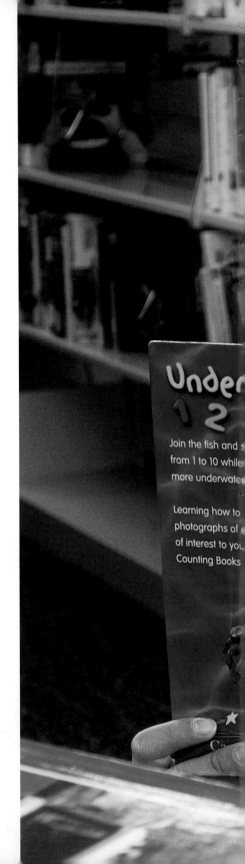

Glossary

library card—a card with a person's name and library number printed on it; people use library cards to borrow materials from the library; they promise to bring back the materials on time and in good shape.

materials—the items at a library that people can read or check out; magazines, newspapers, videos, CDs, tapes, and books are library materials.

research—to look for; library visitors look for book titles or certain subjects on computers.

scan—to use a machine that passes a beam of light over the code on a library card

storytime—a time when children and adults gather to listen to a story read out loud

Read More

Greene, Carol. *At the Library.* Chanhassen, Minn.: Child's World, 1999.

Johnston, Marianne. *Let's Visit the Library.* Our Community. New York: PowerKids Press, 2000.

Radabaugh, Melinda Beth. *Going to the Library.* First Time Read and Learn. Chicago: Heinemann Library, 2003.

Internet Sites

FactHound offers a safe, fun way to find Internet sites related to this book. All of the sites on FactHound have been researched by our staff.

Here's how:

1. Visit *www.facthound.com*

2. Type in this special code **0736823948** for age-appropriate sites. Or enter a search word related to this book for a more general search.

3. Click on the Fetch It button.

FactHound will fetch the best sites for you!

Index/Word List